MW01049382

The Fruit of Love and Grief

To Anne-Marie —

With profound gratitude for your generous support in making this book a reality, reminding me that the ordinary is indeed amazing!

poems by

T. J. Harrison

Finishing Line Press
Georgetown, Kentucky

To Anne-Marie

The Fruit of Love and Grief

Copyright © 2018 by T. J. Harrison
ISBN 978-1-63534-495-0 First Edition
All rights reserved under International and Pan-American Copyright Conventions.
No part of this book may be reproduced in any manner whatsoever without written
permission from the publisher, except in the case of brief quotations embodied in
critical articles and reviews.

ACKNOWLEDGMENTS

These poems, some in earlier versions, have appeared in the following
publications:

Cottonwood: "Insomnia"
Inscape: "Bleeding Heart," "Fidelity," "A Poem For The Way We Are Today,"
"Wilderness of Soul"
Sojourn: "August"
Saint Ann's Review: "Signing the Organ Donor Card"
Southern Poetry Review: "My Grandmother's Lesson In Watercolors"
Third Coast: "Fortune Cookies"
Wisconsin Review: "Opening the Summer House"

Quotation from *The Little Prince* by Antoine de Saint-Exupéry, translated by
Katherine Woods, © 1943 Harcourt Brace Jovanovich, Inc.

Publisher: Leah Maines
Editor: Christen Kincaid
Cover Art: Reid Harrison
Author Photo: Ann Dean
Cover Design: Elizabeth Maines McCleavy

Printed in the USA on acid-free paper.
Order online: www.finishinglinepress.com
also available on amazon.com

Author inquiries and mail orders:
Finishing Line Press
P. O. Box 1626
Georgetown, Kentucky 40324
U. S. A.

Table of Contents

For Vic, Reid, & Royce

Bleeding Heart

Because you wear your heart upon your sleeve,
the crows at least will not go hungry. Leave
the door ajar, the windows open. Meat
is meat after all, and none so salty sweet
as that raw, tender fruit of all you love
and grieve for. Unbutton your cuff, remove your glove
and let them feast. Think of it as just deserts,
or a fitting tribute to all those stained shirts
in your closet. It might hurt like bloody hell
but it won't kill you. You'll have a story to tell
at parties. How hungry flocks, when they finally land,
are nourished not in the bushes, but in your hand.

Insomnia

Gradually now the wind rises, like the sound
of stiffly rustling bedsheets, or pale, dry
leaves scuttering from the eaves of the house.
Always it is the dead of autumn, these hours
skeletal and lean as emptied stalks, miles
from water or the promise of a rain,

though ones who sleep perhaps might dream of rain,
and dreaming be awakened by the sound.
On the county road a pickup thunders past. For miles
its muffled drone lingers in the dry
clumped weeds of the shoulder. You have lain for hours
listening as if to nothing, to this house

sigh and sink in on itself. Even to the house
you are a stranger, foreign as a rain
which threatens but does not arrive. In these hours
abandoned by everything but sound,
anticipating nothing but the dry,
slow whistle of the 3:15, the lost miles

come back to you. You'd forgotten those miles,
that dark river between you and the house,
you and the man you lie beside, but in this dry
interval before dawn, the memory of rain
moves in to remind you. A steady sound
whispers, this, this is the life you have chosen. Hours

mean nothing to the insomniac. Hours
are merely a space to be gotten through, just miles
of clear darkness punctuated by sound
where nothing changes. Listen to the house,
deeply silent as a winter rain,
and to the stiff, bleached shirts snapping dry

on the lawn. Hear the weather vane creak as its dry
iron arrow follows the hours,
like a hired man scanning the horizon for rain.
And know that nothing will help you. The miles
of dark lead always to this life, this house.
Know that you too will hear the nightingale's sound

become the lark's. And when with dawn the miles
dissolve, you too must rise and go forth from this house
into the dry and empty hours without a sound.

Mourning Dove

She has made her nest in the hanging fern,
though for a time I did not see her,
and even later thought her merely lost
or searching it for food.

All the times I watered her nest
not knowing she was there,
still nothing I have done,
no well-intentioned clumsiness
has provoked her to abandonment
or flight. So firm is she
in her belief that I
am not a threat to her.

Perhaps it is as my brother claims,
that they can make a home of anywhere.
But the way she has come to me,
arriving as if by chance,
slipping for no reason
into my days,
as smoothly as a river trout
from behind a stone,
she may be that one blessing
which comes at last to
each of us. The one
we cannot possibly deserve.

For she has come
not to answer any prayer
or ask some promise of reform
but simply to regard and mourn,
if she does mourn,

the passing of all things
equally,
able to find in each
its merest loveliness.

She is the blessing of the presence
of herself alone.
As wind from the sea
on a day in hot summer
might reach far, far inland.

Bringing with it the cool
and tranquil expectation
that here I may yet
make a home
where I had never hoped
to find one.

Fortune Cookies

1.

Friends long absent
are coming back to you. . . .

arms full of flowers,
white chickens strutting in the yard.
Fresh curtains hang
in windows whose casements have,
just this morning,
been flung wide
in sunny welcome.

You will at once recognize
the places
in each other's lives
where you have always
lived.

After all this time.

Empty baskets on the stoop
brim with possibility
of what they yet
might hold.

2.

You are a traveler at heart;
there will be many journeys. . . .

down narrow cobbled streets
of cities with
unpronounceable names,

through warm nights wild
with ripe persimmon,
and the sweaty tang of lovers
rough and dauntless.

How startling the view
as you move
through the foreign country
of each day.

Amazed at the ordinary.

Raised up in awe
by each improbable sojourn,
as a piece of colored glass
to the light.

3.

Good health will be yours
for a long time. . . .

Still, even for you, in the end
is the end.
Dusk falling late,
but still falling.

Of all the things you've loved,
some are gone, some remain.
Leave behind the fear
of going, of being
left behind.

You have come so far.

Now follow the silken thread
of your remaining days
into that vast,
imperishable darkness,
brilliant with stars.

Signing the Organ Donor Card

Now that you've consented to it
there is no going back.
You accept the idea of death
like a package sent c.o.d.
In your mind you review the list
of every possible exit
that would leave organs intact:
the cerebral aneurysm, the midnight
assault, the head-on collision.
What end have you not
already suffered
in your darkened imagination?
What grim possibility
has not been examined
as a potential outcome?

Now anything could happen.
And when it does,
what will become of you?
This sum of parts
never again to be
a greater whole.

What if, in fact,
this is all the immortality
you can hope for?

Say that it is.

Say too that nothing is forgotten,
that what survives,
survives with the history of itself
intact. Each organ then
set adrift to bear

its singular remembrances
into an unknown province.
Each to make its own
and long way
home.

One July day
a farmer in western Iowa
gazes at a picture of the sea
and his heart at once beats faster,
the heart now of a true sailor.

So even without you,
still it may be possible
for your eyes at last
to recognize
the one thing
they were looking for.

For your skin
to shiver with knowing
at a touch
long longed for
in an unfamiliar country.

And for a language,
which to you
was far and foreign once,
to now
be understood.

Tracing Your Own Origins

Hold a shell
the color of flesh
the weight of bone
to your ear

Find in it
where the sea begins

As sound only

A Mind of Winter

All day I've watched the measured fall and rise
of flocks above the headland. It is still
mid-August, and yet blooming in their dark
geometry is the descent of winter
and the tangled lure of something that I own
which has been lost to me. Is this the place

that is home to them, these birds, or just the place
of some presaged departure? How the rise
of wings arouses wild dreams of flight, my own
desire to be elsewhere, even though the still
things, passive as the loom of winter,
are what claim me. As with the gathering dark

of late summer, I've lived anticipating the dark
forgotten ends of things, and each new place
I've looked on always with an eye toward winter,
the way at night I watch for the sleeping rise
of my daughter's chest to suddenly go still,
though it never does. What is ever our own

but such seasons as this of our own
making, the perennial bloom of the mind's dark
orchids. It will be years from now and still
the August flocks will look the same, this place
unchanged, and all the old forebodings rise
undiminished, harbingers of winter.

Still, this is what it means to have a mind of winter.
That I carry with me the snow of my own
absence, though all the while desire to rise
in bright elation as spring sap through dark
branches. If every departure presumes a place
of arrival, where at last will I arrive, if still

I grieve for what I cannot name, if still
the lustrous summer moon becomes in winter
just a milky cataract. What place
will ever comfort me or be my own.
Let me not on this evening, warm as a dark
attic, think of misery, that I may rise

as wings of a single winter bird will rise
in a flight of departure. Some place through the dark
that flight is an arrival, still my own.

Wind from the Sea

It is an unforgiving day in early March.
The ragged winter nearly worn to bone,
has gripped the fields hard frozen since November.
If there is world beyond the brittle moan

of northers, it is unremembered by
the old man breaking ice upon the cattle tank
whose every day is winter in the mind.
Nothing to be thankful for, no one to thank,

for a life in which so much is long gone by.
And days remaining cannot melt the snows
of all he desires that has never come to pass.
In the farmhouse up the hill his wife, too, knows

the bitter haunt of sameness week on week,
the empty chill of old loves lost, like drifts
that linger on the house's shady side.
Each repetitious moment as it sifts

down in regret, falls in but never fills
the deep well of her heart. But then, say
in a sudden turn, the earth is lifted from
its own cold shadow by a gently stray

and warm wind from the sea. A southern breeze
that opens windows into summer where
just for now the worst is all behind her.
The farmer lifts his face and feels in the air

a lightness of departure, as the flicker
of an old elation long obscured
begins to rise. And though he senses colder
days ahead, believes they may yet be endured.

Or say it is a day in late July.
No rain for weeks, nor any hope of rain.
Nor breeze enough to stir the farmhouse hushed
with heat, or prod its sleepy weather vane

in any definite direction. What now
could ever sweep away the dust of so
long settled lives, or fill the absent rooms
with all they might have held? Well they know

the dry spell of the heart that never breaks.
But then an emerald zephyr from the coast
turns the air expectant, though there may
be nothing to expect. How quickly the most

anchored thoughts are set adrift. And while
the drought may continue, the crop may still
be lost, cool portent fills the ripened air.
The old man ponders those who've done him ill,

the grudge of wrongs and injuries his pride
will not release. Perhaps he might forgive
them all. And the farmwife napping after chores
is dreaming of the days still left to live.

The Lamplighter

"The planet now makes a complete turn every minute,"
said the lamplighter, "and I no longer have a single
second for repose. Once every minute I have to light my
lamp and put it out. . . . I always want to rest."
                    The Little Prince —Antoine de Saint-Exupery

For you who can never rest,
sleep is the horizon.
That first star in every evening sky,
the one you wish on.

What is it to know
no matter what you long for,
where you go from here
will be to this place alone.
And the sea of moments
that is your life,
those past
and those to come,
only copy and copy
the same slow ripple
of a desire
never sated.

You think we are
nothing like you,
but who of us does not feel
unlucky,
inescapably compelled
by the things that must be done.
The doing and undoing,
those daily tasks by which
each of our lives
is made necessary.

Sad acolyte,
you believe you are bound
by a duty
you do not desire.
It is not so.
The burden you carry
is of a longing that never sleeps.

That alone
is what keeps you here,
moving
in this haze of wakefulness,
as a dreamer moves
dreaming of himself,

And that horizon you move toward
never closer than this.

August

Moving her body like a slow swimmer
the woman rises. In the middle of the day
she stretches out the blue hours into midsummer
moving her body. Like a slow swimmer
drowning, she turns her face calmly to the day's last glimmer
above the surface of the night. She feels her way
moving her body. Like a slow swimmer,
the woman rises in the middle of the day.

Opening the Summer House

Always now on arrival
we find the rooms open and absent
swelling spectrally in the moldy heat.

Still this is an emptiness we
feed on and follow
as our own bodies hollow out

we settle unalterably into dark
fixed spaces.

How was it
you could drift through rooms

vibrantly astray with life and usher in
the cool blue rain of
five minutes past four.

I always imagined your hands to be
supple, in motion, even
in a vacant room.

Though then of course
there were no vacant rooms.

Fidelity

All this time we have been faithful,
treading the days in tacit synchronicity
as two beasts will pull
instinctively in unison.

Still young,
already we can look back on years
good as a well-mannered child,
as if practicing now
to be called when we are old
an old married couple.

Yet you have never been completely mine.
In all our years of quiet complicity,
there are things you have never spoken of.
And no matter how my body beckons during love,
there is a part of you that will not come to me.

Now we are entering the season
when marriages waver on every brink
for any reason. Tell me
what is worse
than the infidelity which does not happen,
that ecstasy never realized
but always on the verge of occurrence.

I have never dreamed of foreign countries
but of you.
I have never thought of death
but of my life without you.

Please tell me I am foolish.
Please say to me you love me.
Tell me this year, at least,
no raven will fly over the house,
that the wind will not change direction,
but blow warm and gentle
and always from the south.

You Are Lovely . . . Lovely . . . Lovely . . .

The way you scrutinize your body in the bedroom
mirror, I wonder if it's not a damned good thing
Narcissus never made it to middle age. Assume
even his inviolate ego would have felt the sting

of waning muscle tone and crows feet. His sagging pecs
he might have disguised beneath a toga, but what about
that fleshy wattle under his chin. Not even turtlenecks
could've masked those droopy jowls. And unless a drought

were to evaporate the reflecting pool, he'd have had to face
it at some point. Would Echo's constant assurances have been
enough to soothe his fears, and convince him there is grace
in aging. Or would Narcissus have thought her words mere spin

as you do my love, rolling your eyes when I say you look
gorgeous in your new Ralph Lauren. Of course you're not fat.
Don't be silly. You are more ravishing to me than when we took
each other for better or worse. What mirror could reflect that?

Turn away from the glass. No orange and ivory fish that gape
at the pond's surface are more awed than I. My truth
is your beauty now before me—each curve of breast and shape
of thigh, the rippling current of your ever-changing youth.

The Wilderness of Soul

You see, after twenty years
Odysseus did come home,
though by then Penelope
had ceased to expect it.
For a long time she'd had
no memory of his face,
except of having once
remembered it.

No longer did she believe
that anything
could be as it once was,
or hope that what they knew
of each other and of love
would remain unchanged.

This was a different life altogether,
these years spent waiting
for a man she knew
could never return,
even if he should return
to her, it would not
be to her.

So of the life spent with him
and the life spent away,
who is to say
which was the true life, the
essential one,
the one that made
the other life possible.

Seeing her, he knew instantly
he had never journeyed
so far or deep
as the wilderness of soul
before him, as all
the wild world of it
he saw in her.

While she, in turn,
was astonished
not at him,
but at how far she had come
without him.

My Grandmother's Lesson in Watercolors

Arched above the paper
like a diver perched on
some island precipice,
she began the lesson.
This is what she told me.

Once you've chosen a subject
you must open your eyes to it
under water.
And the leaves she painted
were wavery, slow moving,
stirred up
from the bottom of a pool,
as if the water had sung to her,
whispered inside her,
till she herself was bottomless,
overflowing
with ancient starfish.

At sixteen she swam the width
of the Ohio,
the first woman ever,
lured by the borderless
colors of water,
the elusive ones
she might discover there.
Her own strokes fluid
and assured,
she painted the river
with the thin line of her body.
An artist's body made buoyant
with color and with water.

Here, she said,
let me show you.
Look long enough
beneath the surface,
and you will find connections
everywhere. Between
colors and water,
between perspective and water,
between your still unlived life
and water.

Then slowly
she extended her hand to me,
a wild flower blossoming
after a rain.

A Poem for the Way We Are Today

Here with the last light of evening
patching the lawn,
and the way you are today
so precise in its
impermanence,

How is it possible to accept
the passing of now,
the fading slant of July sun,
the sudden sweep of you past me,
a second hand moving
into moments beyond
this moment,

When the way you are today
holds me suspended
in the fragile wonder of what
we already possess.

I have forgotten why
I ever longed for
far-off, unnamed mountains.
And all the ships I've dreamed of
sailing, tonight
under a sifting of stars,
let them embark
without me. I thirst for none
of their fathomless oceans.

I am quenched, as if
forever, by the cool water
of what is.

My most ravenous tigers
sleep now,
sated in the whispering
yellow grasses.

In this deepening heart of summer,
is my every wild hope
tamed.

NOTES

"Wind from the Sea" is an ekphrastic response to Andrew Wyeth's tempera painting of the same name.

The title "A Mind of Winter" is a phrase borrowed from Wallace Stevens' poem "The Snow Man."

T. J. HARRISON was born and raised in Attica, Indiana, and attended Southern Methodist University, The University of Reading, England, and the University of Texas at Dallas. She divides her time between Lawrence, Kansas, and a fourth-generation lake house in Leelanau County, Michigan. An avid oral reader, she makes audio recordings for Audio Reader Network at the University of Kansas, a broadcast and online reading and information service for the blind, visually impaired, and print disabled in Kansas and Missouri.

CPSIA information can be obtained
at www.ICGtesting.com
Printed in the USA
LVHW04s0744180518
577496LV00001B/66/P

9 781635 344950